Book 01

# Hurt No More

## Turn Pain into Purpose

By Hassan E. Munford

Book One: Purpose

**Copyright 2018** *Hassan E Munford*

(www.hemotivates.com) **All rights reserved. No part of this book can be reproduced in any form without the written permission of the author and its publisher.**

Book One: Purpose

## Table of Contents

Table of Contents ............................... 3
Dedication: ......................................... 5
Acknowledgements ......................... 7
Introduction ....................................... 8
Chapter I – Discovery ...................... 11
Chapter II – Freedom Writer ............ 22
Chapter III – Who Will Cry ............... 28
Chapter IV – The Audacity to Dream 38
Chapter V – Break the Silence .......... 49
Chapter VI – Shed So Many Tears ..... 53
Chapter VII – Destined for Greatness
................................................................ 56
Resource page ................................... 66

Book One: Purpose

Book One: Purpose

## Dedication:

To my Earth, my Mom you are the reason I HURT NO MORE. It is because of your love, strength, guidance and fun that I have been afforded a space to become who I am today. For that I am forever grateful to God for choosing you as my mother. You are a phenomenal Black Woman who ROCKS! Love you

To my Dad, I am blessed for the space you have provided for me to be me, unapologetically. I've learned so much through your setbacks and comebacks and wouldn't have it any other way. You remind me daily of my namesake, One who makes better. I love and thank you King!

Tiffany, I love you more than words for allowing me to grow into the man I wanted to be, and you needed me to be.

Xyla, I love you my Xy-Boogie. Lets get this bag! Continue to pursue your dreams and never doubt what's possible when you believe in yourself.

To the ancestors that are guiding me, Carl Burnett, Bernice Munford, Donald

Book One: Purpose

Munford and Louise Burnett, I say Ase. I invite you to keep my spirit grounded in the foundation of love, peace and prosperity. Ase

Book One: Purpose

## Acknowledgements

Thank you to my family and friends! Without you, none of this would be possible. Too many to name now but I appreciate and love who you've allowed me to be in this world.

Book One: Purpose

## Introduction

I write this book to share how writing has helped me overcome and persist in the face of some of my greatest challenges.

My goal in writing this book is to empower you to shift your perspective on the pains, hurts and challenges you face, have faced and will face. The aim is for you to begin to see purpose in any and all of your pain. Each challenge you face is an opportunity for growth in your journey.

Think about it. We have the power to chose how we view adversity. We have the option to allow pain to control our life or the decision to use that pain to find meaning. One of the quotes that has grounded me in believing I am my own rescue states that life is 10% Action and 90% reaction, therefore the focus shifts towards how I react or respond to each moment of hurt.

I chose to use the cover picture of myself as child to illustrate the

# Book One: Purpose

innocence, fearlessness, and greatness we are born with. But through out life's journey, we learn what pain is. Some of us grow into adults with some of the pains we learned as children. And oftentimes if that pain is left undealt with, it manifests in our lives and influences the choices we make daily. So, my daily choice is to choose to HURT NO MORE. I choose to use every pain I learned as a child to find purpose in it in order to help our youth today. And today, as an adult, I seek to use moments of pain to discover a new strength in myself.

At the top of 2019, I discovered the image and symbol of the Sankofa bird. This would be the representation of my year. The Akan believe the past serves as a guide for planning the future. To the Akan, it is this wisdom in learning from the past which ensures a strong future.

So, today I write this book as a way of returning to my past to unlock an even greater future. I am going back and getting all that I left due to the pain of thinking and feeling that I

## Book One: Purpose

wasn't enough. I encourage and invite you to also go back and get your greatness because you too are enough. If there has ever been a moment when you felt you lost a part of you, or felt stuck, it's not too late to HURT NO MORE and TURN PAIN INTO PURPOSE. Please, repeat after me, I AM MY OWN RESCUE

Book One: Purpose

> "Cry, Jay Z, we know the pain is real
> But you can't heal what you never reveal
> What's up, Jay Z?
> You know you owe the truth to all the youth
> That fell in love with Jay Z" - Jay Z

## Chapter I – Discovery

In 2014, I declared that I would not stay somewhere I was unhappy. I began coming into work later and later and most of my time at work, I was daydreaming about what my future could look like. It was ironic that I was sitting at the computer typing my resignation only months after receiving the New Jersey Juvenile Detention Association's, Educator of the year recognition in Atlantic City at NJEA. I had outgrown my back-up plan and my dream was evolving feverishly.

For the past decade, I was empowering young boys and girls to

## Book One: Purpose

use education as liberation as a substitute teacher at Sojourn High School. Sojourn is an alternative program located in Newark N.J., inside the largest juvenile detention center in the state. It was there, in detention, where I found my dream of becoming a motivational speaker and transformation coach. So, I most definitely felt guilt for wanting to part ways with the young people who helped me to discover my purpose. But if I wanted to really be an example of what is possible when you dream big, then I had to listen to my inner guide when it said this mission here was complete. I wanted to do more work in prevention so that so many young black boys didn't end up making poor choices and landing themselves in the system of incarceration. It was time to make a firm decision.

I wrote several more resignation letters before finally submitting my resignation (for the second and final time which you'll learn later) in late 2015. I didn't have another job, but I had a plan. I had faith. I started my own company,

Book One: Purpose

hemotivates.com with a vision of speaking life and transformation into audiences of students and educators. Within the first month of the new year I landed my first paid speaking engagement which, to me, was a sign that I made the best decision for my future. I decided to HURT NO MORE!

Although I hadn't finished my college degree and I wasn't at all equipped financially to start a business, what I was in control of was my emotions, feelings, thoughts and actions. I had the control to change my situation. How could I empower my young people to dream of the life they desired, despite their challenges, if I was not actively pursuing my dream? I also wanted to people of all ages to see that its never to late to change lanes or shift careers. But I had to first have the courage myself to jump

I took a risk. A risk that had me withdraw my retirement fund and spend over $10,000 in the next two months trying to survive. My energy was beginning to feel defeated as things weren't going as planned. I

Book One: Purpose

didn't receive many more paid speaking engagements and soon the passion to be an entrepreneur began to fade. Should I have just stayed somewhere I was safe, yet unhappy?

Even though I had finally put some action into my dream I was about ready to give up. Then, an opportunity popped up in my timeline on Facebook which would be in perfect alignment to who I envisioned myself becoming.

Today, I am employed with The Future Project as a Dream Director, a transformation coach dedicated to you and your dreams for the future. I walked by faith and not by sight. And I walked in my belief that there was more in store for me, but I had to really and truly believe it for myself.

As a result of being a Dream Director, I have created opportunities for the past three years where young people are exposed to possibility thinking. Ive coached young people to lead projects that empower their school community and transform students through developing mindsets and skillsets that move

# Book One: Purpose

them forward. What I think Ive been most successful at with my Dream Team of leaders is allowing them the space to discover themselves while finding community. The young people I work with have become a family who encourage each other and are committed to finding solutions to enhance the culture of their schools and the value of their lives.

In this position, I've been able to travel to places like San Diego, Detroit, The Hamptons, Connecticut, and other places all in the name of growth, transformation and possibility. I'm able to be a dreamer in action so that I may model to my dream team what possibility looks like. I'm living the life I dreamed of those days I was unhappy.

Another recent time that my life looked unrecognizable was being a lead facilitator for our nation-wide Future Camp. Where for three intense, fun-filled, transformational days, students join over a hundred other young people from their community for an experience unlike any other. Future Camp is a chance to jump into

## Book One: Purpose

action to build the life and world that you want. Not only was I chosen as a lead facilitator but my city, East Orange, N.J. was selected as the city to launch the camp. For three days, I was able to live in my power and purpose of developing young leaders from my community, to believe in their greatness. We cried, we laughed, we dreamed, and we danced.

I was personally invited to Louisville, Kentucky for the 2018 Rumble Young Man Rumble Convening by CEO Shawn Dove of CBMA, Campaign for Black Male Achievement because of the work I do in empowering young people. None of this would be happened if I didn't decide to HURT NO MORE.

My life is in alignment with who I want to become. I am living in my fullest potential and beyond grateful for who I am today. I own my own company where I am developing my workshops and thankfully, I am receiving more paid invitations to speak.

Lastly, because my passion for the work I do shows, I was invited to

Book One: Purpose

be on the board of managers for the YMCA in my beloved hometown of East Orange. What better way to give back to the city that helped me develop into the man I am today?

But the decision to HURT NO MORE is a constant, consistent, daily affirmation that grounds me in moving my life forward. It takes a dedicated mindset to be Hassan Eugene, the motivator, the coach. I have always been the fun, outgoing positive guy on the outside but life on the inside hasn't always been that great. You see for years I suffered in silence due to an uncontrollable circumstance that happened in my past. I doubted myself because the world wasn't showing me people like myself. Privately, I struggled with depression and issues of self worth for many years.

Many of you may not know that before I had the courage to speak to crowds and motivate audiences and much before I began coaching young people to break out of their shell , I had a high level of doubt, hurt, pain, shame and confusion that left me

## Book One: Purpose

voiceless so for years. Throughout high school, college and into adulthood, I wore a mask. A mask that everything was alright, and life was good. I wore the mask so well that friends came to me for advice and were inspired by my positive spirit for life. I became so good at wearing the mask that no one could see there were nights I cried and asked God why did he do this to me?

You see, at a young age I was sexually assaulted. An adult had abused their power in a sexual way by striping me, a child of my innocence. And because of this one incident it led me to believe that I was damaged. I had body issues, self esteem issues and low self-confidence but that was private me, that only I knew. I had false expectations of what a man, a young black man was supposed to look like, act like and be like. All I saw was that men were tough and able to get over things, but this wasn't something I could get over.

I couldn't really see myself as a whole person because of what had happened to me. I would never be

## Book One: Purpose

good enough despite succeeding socially in high school and growing into an even more popular young adult. I lived with a constant pain lingering inside. Did people know what happened to me? Were my friends telling people what happened to me? Was I being judged? I grew into an adult who was good at listening to and holding space for others. But most of all, I grew into an adult who knew how to mask pain. I took care of everyone else, but me. in high school I was voted most popular, but I felt most alone on the inside.

I was nothing like my friends. The girls wanted them and not me. And I knew it was all because of what I had been through. Even if they didn't know it, I felt like I was wearing it to school like a uniform. The feelings of incompleteness plagued my thoughts constantly.

Even with the best support system of a large, tight knit family and great friends, none of that seemed to matter or eradicate the hurt from what happened. I had to learn that the abuse I experienced,

## Book One: Purpose

could not control another moment of my time thoughts or energy.

It took me countless days and many failed opportunities to arrive at the peace I live with today. But over time I began to release the story of hurt and increase the story of hope. I had to learn that my past was a place I can refer to, but I could not live there. I could not keep asking myself, Why me?" What I'm committed to today is finding purpose in my past so that I may share how I've learned to manage, process and use my pain as fuel to persevere through adversity.

I was my first student, my first client. I had to coach myself into being enough. I had to coach myself that my future deserved more time than I was spending on my past. I had to shift my mindset. I realized that one uncontrollable irresponsible violent act perpetrated by an adult male did not determine who I was. I was then able to speak my pain, to break my silence. I was learning that who I wanted to become was greater then who I had been and what I had been through. I couldn't let what

## Book One: Purpose

happened to me define me. I had to make a conscious choice to heal

I was so worried about who I wasn't in comparison to others, that I didn't notice who I was becoming. I didn't notice the strength in the system of support I had and still have. What about the kids and adults in pain who do not have any level of support? Who and what are they becoming?

Through the pain, tears and silence, I discovered that I had the power to write my story from a place of victor and not victim. I learned to release the shame and increase the pride of discovering a way to get free.

My mentor, (in my head) Lisa Nichols, said, "My conviction outweighs my convenience." So, yes, it is a challenge to revisit some uncomfortable memories, but I am dedicated to healing a hurt while empowering others to do the same. I've found purpose in motivating myself and others to get into radical action of doing the self work to begin to heal, so that they may find more joy, more peace, more forgiveness

Book One: Purpose

and more hope, in order to live our greatest lives while here on earth.

You have the power to shift the narrative and write your best chapter yet and it all begins with the decision to Hurt No More. You are your own rescue.

**"Ocean views, Small circle it's a chosen few. I wrote it down and I followed through.".**

– Nipsey Hustle

Chapter II – Freedom Writer

Have you ever been stung by a bee? Ever gotten a Splinter? As a child I remember the game of seeing how many berries I can pick off the sticker bushes before I was stuck with a thorn. I learned early in life that the

## Book One: Purpose

only thing that could relieve that pain of the thorn, was time.

The thorn or the pain that I was dealing with wasn't the sexual abuse that had happened to me, rather, it was more so the pain of silence. And what I needed in order to heal, was time. Not being able to talk about it was far greater and affected many areas of my life. To experience such a traumatic event at a young age created shame and there were not many spaces to discuss this. It was known in many black families to be a taboo, something we just don't talk about. My mother did a great job of making sure she lifted me up all my life. I remember the long conversations she would have with me, in the bathroom, as a child making sure I knew I was loved immensely but there were some things that were too painful to talk about to anyone.

And that's when I turned to writing. Writing became my outlet to heal and process some of the things I couldn't speak about. Writing was the tool that would be my therapy. My

Book One: Purpose

safe space. Whether it was ever shared with someone or not, didn't matter, it was my way to break my silence.

Throughout the 80's in the 90's we didn't have cellular phones, the internet, blogs and websites, we had newspapers, magazines and conversations. Most of the homes that I have grew up in always had a Jet, Ebony or Essence magazine and later Black Enterprise business magazine. It was mostly my mom or my aunts that made sure to have literature in the house that reflected black culture and represented professional people living successful lives. The print publications shared stories of people who looked like me and stories of how they built their lives to be successful

Sitting on the couch, I began to read an Ebony magazine and there was an advertisement that stood out to me. They were looking for African-American writers who told stories of overcoming the odds. It was at that moment, that my story had become clear to me. I was overcoming the odds. I was standing in my power

## Book One: Purpose

even if I was standing afraid at this point.

At this point, it's early 2000's and I was doing pretty well for myself as a young adult. I had my own apartment a pearly white Ford Expedition truck, a job with the city and I was making more progress with the ladies. This was important to me because due to the abuse I had experienced, I had intimacy issues with women. I was always nervous and anxious but mostly I was afraid of rejection, so most girls were easier to just have as friends than try to date. I began to become more comfortable with myself and began to realize I was moving through my pain. I was persevering. But in this moment, reading the ad in Ebony, I wanted to move from surviving to thriving. I wanted to be one of those black professional people in the magazine's that I read about who were illustrating that it was possible to go through a challenging experience and still WIN!

So, afraid and nervous, but ready to thrive, I wrote, and I wrote, and I wrote. Then I outlined my story,

Book One: Purpose

structured the climax and I wrote until I felt competition. It was my first call to action, and I entered the contest.

What I was learning through character development was that I had the power as a writer to change the outcome of the story.

As I begin to write, it led to me to research more about men overcoming sexual abuse. I sought out books, people, and places that all pertained to my experience. I was learning I wasn't alone. As challenging as it was to go in Barnes and Noble's and look for books on recovering from childhood sexual assault, I did it. My stomach was turning, I was sweating but I wasn't turning back. I had to endure these difficult moments in order to grow. I began to overcome my fear of worrying that I wasn't enough or that I was damaged, and I began to understand and appreciate that I was just how God made me to be. I wasn't damaged or ashamed anymore, I was human. I was healing.

I think this might be the first time that I was introduced to what

# Book One: Purpose

anxiety is, waiting for the response from Ebony magazine. But in all actuality, I had already won 1st place. I was free. My silence was broken

Even though, keeping it real or keeping it 100, as my young people say, I wanted to win the contest but what I discovered was through me being able to write about my experience, I was peeling off layers and layers of hurt. Writing was empowering me to realize, I was my own rescue!

I was my own rescue because I didn't choose to lean into the negative thoughts dancing in my mind. The thoughts now as an adult about revenge, the culpability, the rage, the anger, the confusion, the loneliness and the times when life didn't seem worth living.

Writing was the key to my self-development and that key allowed me to unlock my power to control my narrative.

Through writing my story and sharing, others began to tell me their stories of abuse. Some confided in me

Book One: Purpose

as being the first person they ever felt safe enough to even say that they had been abused also. These were men, women, boys and girls. I found the power to change my life, my outcome through writing a different ending. And because of my discovery in writing and courage to share, others were also beginning to start a healing process of their own.

**"It's impossible for scientists to make up the seas, to make up the trees
So why we turn our backs on the truth?
It's heaven or hell, the point we seem to hide from the youth."**

**- Scarface**

Book One: Purpose

## Chapter III – Who Will Cry

I couldn't turn my back on my truth as it was evolving. The truth was I was finding heaven in writing my story, but I also found hell in sharing my story prematurely.

After writing my story I had what was known as mental breakdown and was hospitalized in a mental health ward of Mountainside hospital. There, I was checked for manic depressive and bipolar disorder, but the diagnosis was PTSD, Post Traumatic Stress Disorder. Holding back for so long and then sharing so publicly created an uneasy space for me. I felt so free that I was now writing dangerously. The freedom of sharing took a major burden off my back and I had even lost 55lbs working out at the gym. I was FREE. But in the evenings, I was writing with little time for sleep.

At this time, I was working for East Orange Water Commission and going to Bloomfield College, but I was now entering into a phase of life where I wanted to be doing the things

## Book One: Purpose

that were bringing me joy and not just going on with what was expected in life. And college was expected.

You were supposed to work goto school and be happy to enjoy life. But after learning the power writing held for me, I was only focused on re-writing my own story.

So too much writing, working out and not enough sleep landed me into a breakdown. While hospitalized I began to learn who my truest friends were, and I was learning how to have conversations about my feelings surrounding what happened to me. It was my first time as an adult to have some of these conversations with family about the silence I had been suppressing. The worst part was one of my best friends also used what happened to me against me in a heated argument

Through my breakdown, I was also having a breakthrough. I was learning how to find my voice again.

I returned home and eased back into the routine of normal life in order to show I was normal again. Of

### Book One: Purpose

course, there were the rumors I went crazy, but I was learning how my culture responded to pain, healing and therapy.

Mike Lew wrote in his book, *Victims No Longer*, "Our culture provides no room for a man as a victim. Men are simply not supposed to be victimized. A 'real man' is expected to be able to protect himself in any situation. He is also supposed to be able to solve any problem and recover from any setback. When he experiences victimization, our culture expects him to 'deal with it like a man.'"

    There were so many stigmas around mental health. Many black families saw therapy for crazy people and so did I at one point. Highly medicated and seeing a therapist who I didn't connect with, left me feeling like all the progress I made with writing was a waste of time. I felt like the superpower I discovered quickly turned to kryptonite. With the help of my support system, I was able to move through this time of my life knowing I had love from enough

## Book One: Purpose

people who wanted the best for me. And that was important.

Soon I was back in the swing of things and doing what appeared to be living a normal life.

I had been laid off from my city job with the water department along with others due to downsizing and still dreaming of this life of something greater, I was still writing but I dared not tell anyone or share my writing because of what happened the last time. I would journal my thoughts, dreams and feelings towards the past and present but most excitedly, I wrote about my future.

A few months went by and unemployment was running out when I got a call about a position as an instructional aide at Sojourn HS, an alternative high school servicing the detainees of the ECJDC. The Youth House as we called it and Juvee is what they call it today. Hesitant at first but my friend's mom was persistent that she thought Id be a great example for the young men housed there,

## Book One: Purpose

The irony of taking the position was that they wanted me to be the gym teacher. All my triggers flared up of not being enough. Steeped in the low self esteem body issues because of what I had happened to me, I knew this position would challenge me. But here again, I was learning to HURT NO MORE.

    These were the challenges and times that I really began learning what it meant to hurt no more. It meant that every time a challenge showed up and took me back to the trauma I experienced as a child, I had to shift into a mindset of victor and not victim, in order to grow forward. I acknowledged that this past pain was showing up, I processed my choices and decided to accept the challenge to move forward, move through it. SO, through some good self talk I reassured myself that I didn't have to be a fit, in shape gym teacher to do the job, I just had to step up to the challenge and grow.

    Plus, it made it somewhat easier to accept the challenge being that I was maintaining my weight loss.

## Book One: Purpose

I learned a lot about myself and mental health during my recent breakthrough, excuse me breakdown. So, a routine of exercise and designing lessons for health class would be fun for us all. I used different approaches through video's, documentaries and icebreakers. Although I was a substitute, it was important to me put some intention towards lessons empowering these young men and a small number of young women to use education to mentally liberate themselves while being detained.

We were all growing together. It was here that I was teaching but also learning. I was learning that many of young men had also experienced deep levels pain and their pain was influencing their poor decision making. Many of the teachers complimented me on the relationships I built with the young men and said that I had a gift.

What they saw as a gift was merely me holding space for others, like myself, suppressing their pain. While their pain may not have been

## Book One: Purpose

from sexual abuse, they were most definitely, in pain. It was like poem I memorized from the movie, Antione Fisher, which was film closely related to a real-life story about a Black man who persevered through childhood sexual abuse. The poem, by Antwone Fisher, reads:

> *Who will cry for the little boy?*
> *Lost and all alone.*
> *Who will cry for the little boy?*
> *Abandoned without his own?*
>
> *Who will cry for the little boy?*
> *He cried himself to sleep.*
> *Who will cry for the little boy?*
> *He never had for keeps.*
>
> *Who will cry for the little boy?*
> *He walked the burning sand*
> *Who will cry for the little boy?*
> *The boy inside the man.*
>
> *Who will cry for the little boy?*
> *Who knows well hurt and pain*

Book One: Purpose

*Who will cry for the little boy?*
*He died again and again.*

*Who will cry for the little boy?*
*A good boy he tried to be*
*Who will cry for the little boy?*
*Who cries inside of me.*

I felt like I was crying for the little boy in me and for all the little boys/brothers I was teaching. And when the tears were done, there came vision, came purpose. I looked at each juvenile as if that could have been me. I could've easily allowed my pain to encourage me to make irrational and unsafe decisions but instead I had suppressed my pain. So, I empathized with the students and strived to show them that I cared about who they were and not their mistakes. And, more importantly, I cared about who they wanted to become.

    I grew into a teacher, coach, brother, friend and motivator. I also began to break out my own shell and started using my writing for small

## Book One: Purpose

plays we performed. You could find me as Pastor Munford in one play and Rick James in another. I would host events and through this safe space, I was finding a new voice.

The freedom I had gained through writing my story was that my life was changing. Like, literally and practically changing before my eyes. The pain and hurt were shedding layers and the person with purpose was evolving like Tupac's lyrics, A rose that grew through concrete. I began to make more choices based off what I believed now since breaking my silence and who I now saw myself becoming.

The things I wrote about in my story for Ebony magazine were very similar to how my life was unfolding or should I say unpacking? As I unpacked my past, my present was transforming and all through the power of writing.

This had to be around the time I first saw The Secret and discovered the transformation coach Lisa Nichols. In the film, she discusses how thoughts become things. Whether negative or

# Book One: Purpose

positive, what you do with those thoughts will ultimately design how you live your life. In that moment, that was confirmation for me to continue to think of myself as a survivor on a journey of self-development with hopes of one day sharing my story to inspire and motivate others to push through their pain.

Book One: Purpose

## "All I need is one mic" - Nas

### Chapter IV – The Audacity to Dream

During my growth and self discovery at Sojourn, an opportunity of a lifetime came into play. The more I decided to let go of my past, I began to lean more into my future and all the possibilities of who I could become. I remember it vividly. My cousin had an opportunity for with an independent record label for a director of marketing and promotions. He told me what he knew and asked me to stop by the studio to learn more and meet the owner.

Now, what so important to note is that I had always had a dream of singing. Growing up in Doddtown a middle-class neighborhood in East Orange, we'd walk down Linwood Pl on our way to McDonald's singing Always and Forever or Troop's All I Do. Chop, Donald and I thought we were a group. But as we grew from middle school to high school singing

## Book One: Purpose

wasn't popular and street culture was, but we'll save that for another book. But having a chance to be closer to one of my unspoken childhood dreams was a sure indication of what was possible now that I was free from the silence I held as a child.

Ok back to the story

It was a sunny summer day and my uncle had let me take his motorcycle out for the day. I pulled up to the studio in Newark, N.J. on an all black 1200 BMW. Rah came out and opened the gate and let me in. He introduced me to the owner and took me on a tour. This wasn't one of those hole in the wall studios, this was the real deal. Like real deal money was invested. There were two offices, a lounge with leather couches, arcade style video games and flat screen TVs, studio a and studio b with the latest recording equipment. The owner shared his vision, and everything sounded like a dream come true.

For the next few months we were working with different artists, I began using my communications skills from my studies at Bloomfield

Book One: Purpose

College to develop branding for the company while doing different fund raisers to show I could be an asset and soon enough, all systems were a go. Hass The Mayor, Director of Promotions at your service.

    I remember dozing off on a flight to Miami that the label sent a few of us on for The Source Awards. I dreamed of being on the stage crooning some beautiful black queen with my Luther Vandross vocals. She was smiling and blushing, and I was too. While I had made great strides in breaking my silence, I still was working through the fear of failure and rejection. So, instead of mentioning my dream of singing, I played my position and I truly was just happy to a part of a record label. Just as I was about to go into my second verse, the flight attendant tapped my shoulder and said to buckle up, we'd be landing soon.

    I made great networks while in Miami and even secured our artists' music to play in rotation while at an industry networking mixer. Back in Jersey we laughed and talked about

## Book One: Purpose

the fun we had while living our dream of working at a record label. It was back to the grind and business as usual. Work, school, studio. Until one night I came into the studio and heard a crisp young voice bumping over the Mackie speakers.

*"Deep thoughts in the back of my mind, make me get ah attitude, taught myself how to put it in rhyme."* - Hollen Madd

There it was again. Confirmation. Just like the film the secret, this song was a confirmation of just how powerful writing was. It confirmed, to me, your thoughts turned into writing could be used powerfully. The way I interpreted the line was that, the artist had thoughts that were agitating, interrupting, hurting or disrupting his natural view of life so much to the point that he had to do something about it, and he chose to put it in rhyme.

The brotherhood between us grew strong because of our common bond in using writing and music as an outlet to life's adversity. Ultimately, I felt like this situation was going to be

# Book One: Purpose

my ticket to blowing up and making big money so this would be the first time I resigned from Sojourn in 2004 and had the audacity to dream.

    It was during this time I wrote my first song.

>*Ive been hurting so long*
>
>*I don't wanna be alone*
>
>*So Im hear to say*
>
>*This life did me wrong*
>
>*But Im hear to say*
>
>*My struggle made me strong*
>
>*So Im back again*
>
>*Im coming back home*
>
>*And Im here to stay.*

    The importance of sharing this story is that as I continued to unpack my past, I was liberated and free to be who I wanted to be. I was willing to even have conflict and confrontations with my greatest support system. What I was challenged in helping them to understand was that I couldn't return to who I was now that I had

## Book One: Purpose

shared my truth about how the abuse affected me. The abuse violated me, and the silence crippled me from being who I wanted to be, unapologetically, because of fear. But no longer. I learned in my research about survivors of childhood sexual abuse that its critical for the survivor to take back their power. And through writing my story for that contest, I had begun the process of regaining control of my narrative, my life. It was important for me to do the things that brought me joy because for so long I just went with the flow of life and what was expected of me from friends and family because I was stuck at the point where control had been taken away from me.

    The story I wrote was about a singer who was looking for love but had an internal conflict because of his self esteem issues due to sexual abuse.  It was a fiction story about some of my nonfiction experiences and thoughts. The protagonist was written to seem as it was my best friend, but the villain was really the story I had been telling myself all those years of not being enough. It

## Book One: Purpose

was my own internal conflict. And through these new opportunities, in real life, I was getting closer to the character I wrote about but even better I was becoming me.

Back at the label, we worked with some great local and out of state independent artists during that time and I packed up my bags and moved to Dallas Texas for 8 months to promote one of our top selling artists. I was signing more, building with my young brother from another and really feeling like I was living my greatest life. Even seeing more women and having fun dating in a whole new state. Unfortunately, the relationship with the company dissolved after those eight months and instead of moving back home to NJ, I grabbed what I had left in my NJ apartment, told my family my mission and packed a UHAUL up and with $500 in my pocket, to head towards ATL.

Heres why this is chapter is of uber importance. As an adult who had recently become free from silence and had taken back the control, I felt was robbed of me as a child, I had a hard

Book One: Purpose

time accepting that my life was just made for me to accept defeat. While in Atlanta, times were rough. Money was depleting. I was asking friends and family from NJ to order a pizza online to be delivered to me in Lithonia, GA while I waited to hear back from unemployment. I couldn't give up. There had to be something greater. By this time, I had written and recorded a few more songs and gained confidence that I had some decent vocals to be an artist but still not sure if that was who I really wanted to be. But writing music was helping me get through my silence and through my pain. So, it was personal. It was healing. And if I had to risk my comfortability to gain my dream, then so be it, I was finding beauty in the struggle.

    As Im laying in my bedroom on my air-mattress with my 32inch box tv, I hear HollenMadd creating this church like beat. The organs began blaring. DUNN DUNN DUNN DUNN DUNNNNN

    That's when the song, which I named this book after, came to life. I

Book One: Purpose

began to sing from my gut. My life's purpose was all about becoming free from hurt. Tears began to roll down my eyes and it was like a scene from a movie when the words flowed freely

(Chorus)

Don't wanna hurt no more

Don't wanna feel this pain

All I wanna see is the sunshine

No more cloudy days

(Verse 1)

Back in the days on my block

As a kid, Life was so much fun

Didn't worry bout, ever getting older

All we cared about, was pretty girls and soda

But as the years moved on

My life took a difficult turn

Now the world it looks a lil bit colder

Book One: Purpose

And lord I need to lean up on your shoulder

(Chorus)

Don't wanna hurt no more

Don't wanna feel this pain

All I wanna see is the sunshine

No more cloudy days

And all these years I looked so strong

When inside I was slowly dying

Needed somebody that I could talk to

Needed somebody just to understand

That my life has been hard, yeah

Didn't want it this way

I know that HE has a plan

I know that HE will come save me.

(Chorus)

Don't wanna hurt no more

Book One: Purpose

Don't wanna feel this pain
All I wanna see is the sunshine
No more cloudy days
(Bridge)
No more cloudy days
Please take this pain
Away
I've been waiting long and I
Need to see this pain gone

Book One: Purpose

**"Either let me fly or give me death**

**Let my soul rest, take my breath**

**If I don't fly, Imma die anyway, Imma live on**

**But I'll be gone anyday." - DMX**

### Chapter V - Break the Silence

What I was learning while I was healing my pain was that I had control over my life. I was learning what I wanted my legacy to be. My courage was developing through accepting these challenges to grow and it felt like I was destined to walk the path of taking back control at all costs.

My time in Georgia was short lived after breaking my ankle playing football with friends and it was time to return to Jersey. I headed back home and was able to secure my old position at the detention center within the first thirty days.

This time at the detention center, I was tasked at being the permanent substitute for the Literacy

## Book One: Purpose

class and again found, myself creating and designing lessons that were intended to be relatable and relevant to the students I was serving. The difference this time was that I had a new found sense of self and purpose for the work I was doing. I was still building with my music and production and I was also learning how to film and edit videos. I was using my skills and confidence to enhance my position and make an even greater difference in my life and my students.

    One of the counselors at the center designed a week themed towards Breaking Free and asked me to host. Intrigued, I asked more questions about the week ahead. I accepted the invitation and was ready to carry the show as emcee.

    As breaking free week commenced over the next 5 days of the last week of the schools' summer program, I experienced an awakening. The week was dedicated to bringing in speakers and performing plays with students to encourage the young people to break through their pain

## Book One: Purpose

and see promise in their future. As I hosted, I imagined what I would be like as a presenter. What if I had that time to speak, share and inspire? What was awakening was the desire to share my story on a greater level because there were many young boys who had experienced the same trauma that I did as a child.

Over the next several months I began writing a mini-documentary, along with a workshop, that I would ask to present for next summer's breaking free week. I worked hard to write, film, edit and produce what would be my first actual body of work.

*"Break the Silence Before It Breaks You! Make the Write Decision.*

In the film I encouraged the students to use writing, as I did and still do, to overcome adversity. One of my friends/coworkers was so moved by the film that she raised money to purchase and surprise me with a round trip flight for me to be present in Los Angeles for the American Black Film Festival, another contest that called for positive stories of Blacks

## Book One: Purpose

being resilient and overcoming the odds. On the flight to LA, I read all the words of encouragement from the officers, teachers, students and administrators who were all rooting me on. Even the heavy turbulence and uneasiness of the flight couldn't interrupt the ear to ear smile I had on my face. I was living on purpose and in my purpose.

No longer was I timid or afraid to share my story. My story was no longer mines. It was for the boys that were ashamed of what happened to them. I wanted my legacy to be a light in someone else's life because I understood what it meant to feel pain as being an unpleasant feeling or emotion. I found a quote that stuck with me and I used it on the back cover of the mini-documentary that states,

*"Jesus said, If you bring forth what is within you, what you bring forth will save you. But if you do not bring forth what is within you, what is within you will destroy you." - The Gospel of Thomas*

Book One: Purpose

## "Ah, I suffered through the years and shed so many tears. I lost so many peers and shed so many tears"- Tupac Shakur

### Chapter VI – Shed So Many Tears

I understand how difficult it is to return to the root of your pain but imagine what your life can look like when you act opposed to staying stuck. I understand the fear of being vulnerable, but I also know the how taking a risk on yourself, can transform your life into who envision you are. I write this book and find purpose in assisting in holding space for people to transform their own lives because I wish I would've had someone school me earlier. I shed so many tears trying to discover who I was and what I was going through and today I vow not to let those tears go in vain. I wish I would've had the examples of men who experienced what I did with abuse so that I could see there was hope sooner. Maybe then I might've had a different

# Book One: Purpose

perspective and healthy ways to process pain. So, my purpose is to not allow another day pass without sharing how I persevered and how you can too.

    My first day as a dream director we went on a journey through Weequahic park in Newark eating leaves off the trees, doing pullups with a team who helped when you couldn't do it, did Yoga in the grass and all to emphasize our theme for the year. The theme was to become comfortable with being uncomfortable. I know how hard it is to face the fear of being uncomfortable, but I also know that if you do your self-work and take a risk on you, you will succeed. I know what it looks like to have the courage to confront the pain that is holding you back from being the greatest version of yourself you can be because I'm breaking through those same fears as I write this. But I invite you act on writing a new chapter, your best chapter!

    I wish I would've known this sooner and that is my purpose in

Book One: Purpose

writing this book for you. Sharing is caring. The power is in the share not the silence. If I can share, so can you because when one of us wins, we all win. Someone needed to hear my story from me in order to find hope and someone is waiting to hear how you also found purpose in your pain. My purpose as I reflect now is to remember that handsome, fearless young boy on the front cover. If ever I need a reminder to HURT NO MORE, it is because he deserves to walk in his destiny of greatness.

# Book One: Purpose

Book One: Purpose

## "It was all a dream!"
## – Biggie Smalls

### Chapter VII – Destined for Greatness

    This past summer of 2018 I was homesick and missing what I value most and what keeps me comfortable, Tiff, Xyla, Tyson, my home base. Oh, I did tell you that in my story to Ebony, it was a love story, right? Well, as I stated, I wanted to find love and as I began to love myself more God sent me a woman who made my story complete. And a daughter who gives me greater purpose of what it means to be an example, a model for how to live life abundantly. Still not fully sure about my dog, Tyson, just kidding, I love my boy boy.

    But I really wanted to perform at our Passion Show for the Dream Director Summit. The saboteur was showing up, which is my inner ego who likes to keep me comfortable and makes it ok for me to retreat into my shell, But after a good convo with Tiff I got my self together, through on

## Book One: Purpose

some good music and began to get ready for the night.

I think it could've been the anxiety of trying to sing my own song, Hurt No More, for the passion show which was also making me retreat so in true Dream Director principle #6, There's Always Another Way!

While in the shower, where most of my best ideas come from, I had the idea of returning to my high school performance. Instead of singing my song where Id be a bit unpolished, let's go have some fun.

It was lights camera's and action as I pushed past the saboteur and my fears. I was living in my greatness. I rocked the stage with all my future family as we sung Biggie Smalls' "It was all a dream."

The point is that sometimes wave got to be our first client and coach ourselves out of sabotage or misery. Hurt No More is just that. A decision to challenge whatever fear or anxiety arises when our greatness is being tested. We've got to commit to breaking through fear, pain, hurt and

## Book One: Purpose

shame and rise. Hurt no more is an action. It's a mantra and a mindset for me. I know what it looks like to not give up and as a result I am now an author, speaker and coach!

Another one of my favorite songs that sets the mood to motivate me is a Jersey artist from Newark, Redman, *"TIME FOR SOME ACTION."*

**Step 1 - The permission to Dream**

I (say your name) give myself permission to dream.

Speak life over wherever you presently are in your journey. It doesn't matter your race, class, level of education or position in life, we all have the power to give ourselves the permission to dream of a life greater than we ever imagined. Sometimes, our past can limit us and sometimes it is our stories created from our past that limit our belief in our present and future self.

One way that worked for me in discovering my purpose was to create a vision board. After I gave myself permission to dream, I then needed to see what was ahead of me. There are

# Book One: Purpose

many ways to do a vision board so I will let you get creative and tailor yours to who you want to become. My vision board right now has my development center, a book tour and a beautiful home on it. I made my board into a wall in my basement office. Dream big. Small goals for a big victory.

**Write a letter to the child in you**

Inside this letter, I'm asking you to write this letter from a perspective of victor. Tell the child how he/she has survived! Remind him/her of the things they've done despite their hurt, pain and challenges. Help them remember their natural zest for a life of abundance on their terms.

**Step 2 - Decide**

The Action marathon

I was amazed watching my fellow Dream Director's Brit (putayounginyourbudget.com) facilitate a workshop named an action marathon. It basically is what it says. Decide what actions you want to take today that will move you forward towards your purpose. If you don't

## Book One: Purpose

know what your purpose is now, that's ok too, put it on your list. You have the power to decide how your life can evolve. Write down 5 things that you can commit to doing for yourself and when you're done with them, celebrate yourself.

Decide that you will no longer suffer in silence. Whether its writing, seeking therapy or hiring a coach, decide that it's ok to have someone help you process a pain that you may be experiencing or have experienced. Live on your terms as it relates specially to healing. Your outcome is in your decisions. Be gentle with yourself and decide that you have done the best you can do up to this point and that is good enough. Celebrate your survival.

**Step 3 - Declare**

"There's purpose in my past." - Hemotivates

Create a mantra. A mantra, which I understand, is a continuous repeated form of self-talk that helps me in concentrating and meditating on my greatness. What is your mantra? Some

## Book One: Purpose

of the easiest ways to begin a mantra is to start off with, I can, I am or I will. Try to fill in the blank as it relates to the uniqueness of you. Write this down on a sticky note or several and place them where you can see and recite. It's amazing to experience the shift in vibration you can have when a challenge arises through using your mantra. Trust me, I'm living proof.

I teach more about these steps and others in my up-coming online course, Dream, Decide, Be Destined for Greatness. 7 Steps to a New Beginning! In the course, I go even deeper into my story and how I transformed my life.

Today, as a result of the self-development work on myself, I've been able to use 3 steps to transform my life from pain to purpose. It is because of this process that I no longer feel the shame, hurt, or the pain of my past. Today, I coach young people and adults to use their pain as a place of reference and not residence. I'm looking for people who would like to uncover a pain, discover

## Book One: Purpose

their purpose and declare their decision to HURT NO MORE!

I invite you to join me!

In closing, I leave you with this reminder in the form of a poem from my dreamer Taiwo. She wrote and dedicated this poem to me at our end of the year banquet in 2016 and it's been with me in my spirit ever since. Thank you.

>Fear, you scared me to the point where I can't stand on my own anymore.
>
>Doubt, you just keep pushing me around like I'm a nobody
>
>And Failure, you just keep letting me down
>
>I am done
>
>I am done being pushed around
>
>I am done being told what to do
>
>I quit
>
>So hears the news for you
>
>You don't have the audacity to boss me around

Book One: Purpose

So, let there be light

You don't have the right to rule over my life

So, let there be light

Because this person standing here today is not afraid of you anymore

This person right here has already won the battle

So, fear, doubt failure, (pain)

Get behind me because you now work for me

Haven't you heard that through every darkness

A light will always shine through

You can never hide a star

Because no matter what

Its brightness will always emerge

You may pull me in the wrong path

But don't let that fool you

Because no matter where I go in life

I will make it to my promise land

Book One: Purpose

And uh when you see obstacles

Tell them I said

Let there be light

Because the king/queen has arrived

And he/she is ready to take back their throne

I am not that type of person that you used to know

I am not that type of person, ok

I have turned over a new leaf

I am not your hypnotized slave

Nor am I your puppet

Because all you ever said about me was a lie

All you ever said that would become of me, was a lie

Because through that negativity

A leader was born

Through all the demons,

Book One: Purpose

An angel has emerged like a lion's roar

Because within me, there is hope

With hope, there is faith

With faith, there is belief

With belief, there is vision

With vision, there is light

And with light, huh, nothing is impossible,

So, let there be light

# The Law

# The Law

Kevin Wayne Joseph

# Dedication

This body of work is dedicated to my family and friends for believing in my vision and keeping the faith with me. Also to the C/O 2015 of Xavier University of Louisiana for being the underlying inspiration. Thank you all.

*"Faith is the currency of the Kingdom."*

# Contents

| | |
|---|---|
| Introduction | 1 |
| Chapter 1: Obedience | 5 |
| Chapter 2: Faith | 11 |
| Chapter 3: Action | 17 |
| Chapter 4: Association | 21 |
| Chapter 5: Planning | 27 |
| Chapter 6: Confession | 31 |
| Chapter 7: Love | 37 |

Chapter 8: Money        43

Chapter 9: Mentoring        51

Chapter 10: Giving        57

Chapter 11: Expectation        63

Chapter 12: Management        69

# Introduction

As the late Dr. Myles Munroe would say, "God's Word is Law." Every word that God speaks is a governing testament as stated in Matthew 4:4, "…men shall not live by bread alone, but by every word that proceedeth out of the mouth of God." The laws of man can be altered, amended, or discarded completely, while the laws of God are inflexible, immutable, and cannot be changed. These laws are both written in plain sight, and in our very nature. God has intended for everyone to live together in unity, harmony, and to enjoy an abundant lifestyle. God's law

was created to protect, govern, and make prosperous for all mankind. Although our laws may not always line up with His, we should all strive to reach our full potential.

Now, God's laws may elude us if we are not careful and open-minded. Then we may find ourselves asking what are the laws of God? What are they protecting us from? What are they governing us for? Why does God want us to succeed? What is the purpose of these laws for our lives?

God Almighty created all of us to succeed, to fulfill our purposes here on earth. Look at nature and understand, everything was created for success. Some trees produce fruit, birds fly, and fish swim. The success of these are built into their very nature. We ultimately have the same design, our successes are built into our being.

For this book, we will focus on the Bible as a law book and specific passages to relate these laws. Not every one of the laws will be covered, only those in which I am inspired to write about.

There are chapter questions everyone should ask themselves to fully understand the laws and how to use them. They are designed to help pinpoint shortcomings and help achieve self-awareness. Every question may not

impact as much as others, but they are necessary to getting the lessons out of this book.

The Bible tells us that faith without works is dead. After the chapter ending questions, there are action steps to take to become consciously aware of the laws and when they are working.

When I first started writing this book, I was broke, sleeping on a floor in my parent's living room, jumping from relative's sofas to friend's floors, working at a job I had no desire to succeed in. My bank account had been closed on two separate occasions because I carried a negative balance for more than 40 days, and I drove a 2002 Lexus ES 300 with 258,000 miles on it. I dressed and acted as if life was good, but I was miserable and out of place. I was tormented. I always knew I'd be successful, but I was failing at life. Fast forward one year, my life has been transformed. I moved to Los Angeles, bought a new Lexus IS 250, got a job I asked for and am now earning more money than I have ever in my life. I am truly happy for the progress I have made and for the person I am becoming. Life is truly great once you find the keys to a successful life.

-4- | Page

CHAPTER

# 1

# Law of Obedience

*"Of every tree of the garden thou mayest freely eat: But of the tree of the knowledge of good and evil, thou shalt not eat of it: for in the day that thou eatest thereof thou shalt surely die." Genesis 2:16-17.*

When Adam disobeyed God, it was the first law broken, and the entire world paid for it. Laws have consequences; for every action, there is an equal and opposite reaction. Consequences are neither good nor bad, they are simply results of a given action. When God told

Adam not to eat of the tree, it was a command that was meant to protect Adam from dangers unknown to him and from damaging the perfect, harmonious fellowship between God and man. It can be likened to a loving parent who teaches their children not to drink poison or play with fire. Do their parents dislike them and are "sucking the fun out of life?" No, they are simply protecting their loved ones from dangers unknown to them. God wants us to instill His Words into our hearts, because His Words are law and law governs and protects. When morals and values are instilled into a child, the parents are no longer required to teach right from wrong, the laws will govern the child's actions and behaviors.

In the event problems arise, we may be quick to consult God on situations He has already provided answers to. We may not realize it because we have not been taught to learn the laws God has laid out for us. Obedience to the laws of God will guarantee peace, love, understanding, and wisdom in one's life. Neglecting His laws will cause unnecessary heartache.

Growing up, I would often hear adults use the phrase, "Obedience is better than sacrifice." This is something they would say to get kids to wash dishes, fold

laundry, or clean their rooms. As a child, I never understood what it meant and would always picture myself on a cross being crucified if I was disobedient. That phrase originates from 1 Samuel 15:22 where Samuel, prophet of God, is speaking to Saul about his disobedience of God's commandments to destroy the Amalekites and everything they possessed. In return, Saul tries to make burnt sacrifices unto God to please Him, rather than obey His commands. Disobedience caused Saul to lose his place as king and God had Samuel anoint another as king—the shepherd boy, David. Obedience to God's laws are crucial to our success. He knows the path we should take.

In my own life, I have seen the benefits of being obedient to law. When I stopped spending all the money I earned, more money started coming my way. When I began to eat healthier and stayed away from too much fast food, my body got better. I became obedient to law and to what God was telling me to do. I am being obedient in writing this book. I was also obedient in moving to California. Being obedient to divine law will cause your life to move forward in the best direction. At every point in life, we should all ask what are we being asked or told to do. It will all work out for our own good and keep us motivated to pursue our purpose in life. Understand that many avoidable

issues come from being disobedient. It is our parents telling us, "I told you so." I am pretty sure we have all heard this phrase many times. Life seems to go better for those that are obedient and are on the right path. If you are obedient and everything has been going wrong, you should check your path. If you are on the right path, rest in knowing everything works together for the good of those that love Him and are called according to his purpose (Romans 8:28).

If we are not careful in obeying God's words, we will lose out on the good and magnificent things He has for us. Obedience to law will guarantee success in anything we want to achieve in life. Be obedient.

## Chapter Questions

Have you been obedient to the Voice of God lately?

Have you delayed being obedient?

What are some instances in your own life where you were disobedient and it caused trouble?

Did you learn from those mistakes and move on?

How has obedience helped you in your personal life?

## Action

Whenever you get a "hunch" or "inspiration" write it down and act to complete it. God sometimes gives us inspiration and our obedience to act is what propels us forward. Listen carefully whenever He speaks, being obedient can change your life forever!

- 10 - | P a g e

CHAPTER

# 2

# Law of Faith

*"Call things that be not as though they were."*
*Romans 4:17*

The "Law of Faith" parallels the "Law of Expectation". Here we are instructed to believe on those things in which we want to happen in our lives. The Bible states, "Without faith it is impossible to please Him" (Heb. 11:6). Keep in mind we are not referring to religion, but law. Do not mistake pleasing God is merely an act of raising your hands and singing praises, but more so carrying out your divine assignment. Having faith is the

complete reciprocal of being fearful. God is never fearful, He only harbors faith. Remember God did not give us a spirit of fear, but of love, power, and a sound mind (2 Timothy 1:7). God already established the foundations of the world and its law. One is believing in yourself; and your abilities. Another is also believing what He said you can accomplish and who you are, which also requires faith. Furthermore, the Bible states in Jeremiah 1:12 that God watches over His word to perform it. Whatever He said, stand on it, no matter the circumstances, no matter the odds, no matter your current situation. If He brought you to it, He will bring you through it. We must keep reminding ourselves that the Bible is not a religious book, but a law book, containing the laws that will ensure your own success.

In life, we go through difficult times that can sway our faith. We must remember that God promised to never leave nor forsake us. Jesus also gave us instructions on how to get God's power to work for us when facing difficult times. In Mark 11:23-24, the Bible says, *"For verily I say unto you, that whosoever shall say unto this mountain, Be thou removed, and be thou cast into the sea; and shall not doubt in his heart, but shall believe that those things which he saith shall come to pass; he shall have whatsoever he*

*saith. Therefore I say unto you, What things soever ye desire, when ye pray, believe that ye receive them, and ye shall have them."* We must speak and believe on those things in which we desire. Now, what has mostly eluded believers is the act of believing. We assume God's work in our lives means, "resting in Him," or sitting back passively. We wait for God to do magic and make things appear that we may have asked for, failing to take the necessary steps and actions— a violation of divine law. The Bible tells us faith without works is dead. We must also do our part in working toward the goal or ambition in which we desire God to help us with. The work is not as difficult as we make it out to be. We must remember that God's part has already been completed, before the foundation of the world. All we must do is continue to work towards that goal. Believe and succeed!

Through articles, books, and mentors I have read and listened to, it has been said that many scholars, thinkers, and the top five percent of the world agree it is impossible to achieve anything without faith. The faith to believe it can happen. The faith to believe and see the vision as clearly as reading this book. Napoleon Hill, once said, "Whatever the mind can conceive and believe, it can achieve." The word, *whatever*, means there are no

boundaries or limitations, except the ones that are set up in our own minds. We know that an individual will only go as far as they can see in their minds. Oftentimes we doubt we can do great and mighty things, but for some peculiar reason, we believe someone else with similar values, circumstances, and background can reach that level of greatness. Have you ever heard a friend, colleague, or family member tell you they're not able to achieve this or that, but then turns and look at you and say, "You can do it! You have something in you I don't have. It isn't meant for me, but you can do it." The Bible states in Proverbs 23:7, "For as he thinketh in his heart, so is he." Although we may believe some goals are possible for others, we must have faith to believe what we can achieve them ourselves. This verse inspired the book "*As a Man Thinketh*" by James Allen which in turn inspired "*The Secret*" by Rhonda Byrne. To this day, millions have turned to these books to find peace, joy, happiness, and anything they desired to have in life. We must not forget these words are written in one of the most widely distributed books in history. Counting the Bible out is ludicrous as it is the basis for which most success books are written. For any self-help book to be useful, the reader must have faith to act upon

what the book instructs him or her to do, and believe what it says.

Behind every divine law or principle is a promise of a guaranteed result, but behind our feelings or emotions, there are not any promises. Let us use the Law of Gravity for illustration. Even without knowing what the law is or how it works, we can all agree it is acting. The Law of Gravity acts upon everything in the universe. While ignoring the Law of Gravity, a rock is thrown out the top floor of a ten-story building. What happens? Does the rock keep traveling in the manner it was thrown? Or does gravity act on it and eventually bring it to the ground? We know the obvious answer. The same applies to God's Laws, although we may not notice them all the time. They work constantly to shape our realities through the decisions we make. We must be conscious of our choices and actions, because they shape our realities. Believe the laws will bring the desired result of our pursuits, then success shall come. Have faith!

**Chapter Questions**

Think of a time when your faith has gotten you through a difficult situation?

Are you doing what it takes to receive the blessings God has for you by believing?

Do you have faith partners to encourage you through difficult times?

Where do you believe your faith can lead you regarding your life's purpose?

**Action**

The next time you are faced with a difficult situation, keep repeating, aloud, "I am more than a conqueror, I am a winner and I am designed to succeed!" Faith comes by hearing and hearing by the Word of God. Repeat what God has said about you.

CHAPTER

# 3

# Law of Action

*"Even so faith, if it hath not works, is dead, being alone. Yea,
a man say, thou hast faith, and I have works: and I will show
thee thy faith without thy works, and I will show thee my faith
by my works.*
*James 2: 17-18*

Many believers question God about why their lives
are stagnant. They may ask, "Lord, why my life isn't
moving forward? I trust in you, I believe you," and God
says it is because you are not taking action! To use the Law
of Action, set a goal, believe it is possible, and take the

necessary steps to achieve it. Most people have not even set the goal and do not know what they truly desire. If we do not know where we are going with our lives, why are we in a hurry to get there? Without setting a clear path, you can hinder the law from working in your life. Oftentimes, we never set solid goals that will brings forth a clear vision and therefore we go through life without accomplishing anything great or impactful in the world or our communities. The Law of Action requires a plan and action!

Take the life of Jesus for example. The Bible teaches us Jesus began acting on his purpose at age 12. He started teaching in the temple with the scholars of his time and they marveled at how much wisdom and knowledge he had of the scriptures, without any training. You too, no matter what age, can begin acting on your purpose in life. Once we realize our purpose seeks us, we should not worry or be afraid. God has equipped each of us with greatness, not mediocrity, but true greatness!

It has been said that most people die at 25 and are not buried until 65. They never act on their dreams and die with them. Every individual walking this earth is unique and has a specific purpose here on earth. Not acting on our

dreams, what we are born with, what gives us our drive, is an act of committing spiritual suicide. According to Deloitte's Shift Index, a survey was done, and it revealed, 80% of Americans dislike their jobs, because it has nothing to do with their purpose. Most people do not experience a sense of fulfillment and fulfillment brings joy, happiness, love, and comfort. True purpose fulfills our lives. We are here to make a deposit, but we are robbing ourselves, our futures, and ultimately God by not acting on our dreams. Act and watch how your dreams come true!

Today, make a vow to live on purpose, to be proactive in life and not reactive. To change the way your attitude is towards your dream and goals. Keep your ambitions high and frustrations low. It is your time to shine, your time to let the world know you are here and here with a purpose. Act. Live on purpose!

## Chapter Questions

Are you truly happy with your current situation?

Do you feel there is more you can contribute to life?

Have you identified your dreams?

Have you written down your goals?

Do you take the necessary steps to make your dreams a reality?

## Action

The next time you get an idea, immediately begin research on it. Most people never act on their dreams or ideas because they do not know where to begin. Start researching and reading, find out if others are doing something similar and connect with those people via social media or networking events. Do all you can in attainment of seeing this idea a reality, no matter what sector it is in.

CHAPTER

# 4

# Law of Association

*"Be not deceived, evil communication corrupts good manners."*

*1 Corinthians 15:33*

Have you ever heard the phrase "birds of a feather flock together? or you don't get out of life what you want, you get what you are?" Many times, we get caught up in having a good time and think life is going well, while the people in our lives are not prosperous. I was guilty of this. We all want to achieve something great; no one wants to live a mediocre life, but we fail to realize that people in our

lives and our environments affect us greatly. I once heard, "If you have a problem with your life, you should have a problem with the people in your life." Not meaning in a difficult season, but overall an unfulfilled life. With not knowing who we are or where we want to go, we will meander through life, attracting anyone and doing anything. This often leads to abuse of one's life and purpose. We can look around at people in our own families or close friends that are just wandering through life without any direction. I was introduced to *"Outwitting the Devil"* by a close friend, and he always used the phrase, "They're drifting." In the book, the term drifting means to sail through life without a plan, without goals, without a dream. Yet we see people doing just that. Coming out of college, I recall asking my peers what they wanted to do and where they wanted to be. The most popular response was, "I just want to get a job" or "I'm going back to school." Why would they say that? Not that something is wrong with a job, or going back to school, because their dream may require more training, but some never defined what they truly wanted. I was searching for more concrete responses such as, "I am going work here so I can achieve this or I am going back to school so I can accomplish that." In the Bible, you will find in Proverbs 4:23, "Above all else,

guard your heart, for everything you do flows from it." Monitor everyone and everything that enters your life, all influences. Although during our upbringing, we are not aware of our influences, we can decide what enters our spirits now, as responsible adults. Failure to do so can result in a wandering nature or *drifting*. People who do not take control over their lives will always attract people who do not take control over their lives. Right now, take inventory of your life. Exposure causes expansion. Once you are exposed to new ways of thinking, you will attract people that think the same way.

This brings us to another part of the Bible in the book of wisdom, Proverbs 13: 20, *"He that walketh with wise men shall be wise: but a companion of fools shall be destroyed."*

It is up for us to decide who we want to be and what we want to accomplish in life. Once you have discovered those two, you will begin to find individuals who are already where you want to be (mentors) and individuals who are on the same journey as you (peers). It can be quite challenging to find such people. Oftentimes, we find pretenders and quitters; those who talk the talk, but never walk the walk. The world is filled with this kind. As the

Bible says for every tree is known by its fruit, we must look at the "fruit" or the results that be. It will reveal the person and their worthiness.

We should all have friends in our lives to help monitor our actions; our brother's keeper, if you will. Friends that will help us stay on track and unafraid to hold us accountable. Friends that will not tolerate anything but our best. Friends that are unafraid to judge and vice versa. We should be able to do the same in their life. If you do judge, judge righteously and not with a condemning heart. Judge the people around you in a manner that will inform them if the road they're heading down is the right one, according to their dream and purpose. Reminder: you must first identify your dream and purpose and adjust your life accordingly. The small everyday activities you participate in will determine your life's outcome. Focus on creating yourself and learning the tools necessary to become whom rests in your heart, your highest self.

**Chapter Questions**

Who have you been associating yourself with?

Are they promoting or hindering your wellbeing?

Do they encourage your dreams or not?

Are they helpful in your decisions?

Do you see qualities of yourself in them?

Are they the type of people that can help you get to the next level?

**Action**

Monitor your group of friends and how they act. Are they helping move you toward your goal? Are they a distraction? Never listen or read negativity about yourself, it only destroys self-esteem. If your current group is not conducive to your goals, then get more friends that are where you want to be. You don't have to cut off everyone, just talk and hang out less. You want to engage and interact with people that can elevate you.

CHAPTER

# 5

# Law of Planning

*"Commit thy works unto the Lord, and thy thoughts shall*
*be established. A man's heart deviseth his way: but the*
*Lord directeth his steps."*
*Proverbs 16:3; 9.*

Too often people name what they want, but never get around to planning how to make it happen. We find ourselves planning a Saturday night, a birthday, anniversary, or a vacation, but never plan for our lives. From a distance, this seems challenging because it requires the most neglected part of our human nature, our mind. Earl

Nightingale once said, "Our minds can complete any task we assign to it, but normally we use it for little jobs, instead of big important ones." Begin now to use your mind to become your greatest self. There is no shortage of abundance on this earth, whether riches, health, happiness, peace, or mental capacity. We were created to create, build, and occupy earth until He returns. To get to our place of heaven on earth, we must identify what it is, where it is, what it looks like, and who's there with us. This is all a part of the planning aspect of your life. We must first get a mental image of heaven on earth, and then create and execute a step by step plan to reach the goal.

If anyone is having trouble accepting that God created us with a purpose, recall that there is none like Him, He finishes the task and then He begins. The Bible says in Isaiah 4:6, *"I am God, and there is none like me, declaring the end from the beginning, and from ancient times the things that are not yet done."* God already completed the task (our purpose) and now wants us to begin it on the earth. That is the reason why we are born, where we were born, to whom, and the specific time. Remember God never makes mistakes, so everything is perfect, including your life's purpose.

Travel back to Jeremiah 29: 11, *"For I know the thoughts that I think toward you, saith the Lord, thoughts of peace, and not of evil, to give you an expected end."* In other words, God has a plan for your life and your plan should be in line with His for He will provide the best life. Once you have established your relationship with Him, your plans will begin to come to fruition. If anyone does not know where they are going with their lives, any road will take them there. It is very important we take a day, a week, or even a month to devise a plan that will help accomplish our goals.

**Chapter Questions**

Have you identified your Heaven on Earth?

Have you identified who will help you get to your place of serenity?

Where are you going with your life?

When are you planning to get there?

Have you thought about planning for success?

**Action**

Set time apart from your day—you're never too busy to improve yourself—and plan your week. Not a to-do-list, but a goal list and a step by step process on achieving that goal. Then set a new one. This simple strategy will bring you more and more success and you can accomplish in five years what most people don't accomplish in their lifetime. Start getting more intimate with God, He will direct and guide you. Never worry about how, remember to commit thy works unto the Lord and He will establish your thoughts. It is never your business on how, all you need is a goal and faith, leave the how up to Him and allow Him to work on your behalf. Begin today to plan and live the life you dreamed of.

CHAPTER

# 6

# Law of Confession

*"For verily I say unto you, that whosoever shall say unto this mountain, be thou removed, and be thou cast into the sea; and shall not doubt in his heart, but shall believe that those things which he saith shall come to pass; he shall have whatsoever he saith."*

*Mark 11:23.*

In Genesis, God spoke this world into existence. He gave us all that power, the ability to shape our realities with our mouths. Have you ever said something negatively like, "I always get sick or this always happen to me?" Notice

how you tend to get what you say and believe. The best way to get better results is to say and believe what God has said about you. Things like you shall live and not die; You are the head and not the tail; or my favorite, I can do all things through Christ who strengthens me. For He gave me the power to write this book.

Ninety-three percent of all communication is non-verbal and seven percent is the actual words we speak. Knowing this can help us change the center of our speech, our thoughts. The Bible says, *"A good man out of the good treasure of his heart bringeth forth that which is good; and an evil man out of the evil treasure of his heart bringeth forth that which is evil: for of the abundance of the heart his mouth speaketh." Luke 6:45.* Be conscious of your speech. Really focus and pay attention to the words you release and the different situations in which you release them. Circumstances can affect how we speak and the tonality we use. Any words or phrases we speak reflects our current conditioned mind. It is not hard to learn much about a person once we hear their speech. It will reveal more about who they really are than asking for them to talk about themselves.

Be very careful in what you allow to enter your spirit. Constant exposure to anything can and will cause one to conform to the ideologies related to that exposure. Once you believe a thing or it enters your heart and is accepted as truth, you begin to speak it. Notice the conversations in which you engage and the ones in which you abhor. You will notice the ones you engage in are like what is in your heart, what you love. Likewise, with what you abhor, you will despise the conversation and soon separate from the person or persons speaking on it.

The Bible states in *Proverbs 18:21, "Death and Life are in the power of the tongue: and they that love it shall eat the fruit thereof."* You can speak so much trouble into your life by not having the right heart, simply because you may just say something that you have heard others say and accepted it as truth and you get the results in which you seek. Likewise, speak life into any situation you find yourself in. Seek positive motives and people to encourage, build, and motivate you, because they will play a part in your heart's desires and you will speak what your heart is filled with. Take control over your life and your heart. Be a master to your time and resources for they are all governed by your heart and spoken out of your mouth.

I recall hearing the Greek term, *homologeo*, biblically, which can be translated as, *"To say what God has said!"* God only speaks life, He only speaks greatness, He only asks for our best; so why would we think less of ourselves? Why would we think we cannot achieve the dream? Why would we think it is impossible? Impossible is not impossible at all (Impossible = I'm possible). Remember God would not ask you to do anything if you did not have what it takes to get it accomplished.

Speak words of greatness into your life. Speak affirmations and encourage yourself. Always build yourself and others up. It is a part of loving yourself. Learn to love yourself completely and wholeheartedly, even meaning to respect yourself enough to remove yourself from harmful situations. If we truly loved ourselves, would we engage in activities that feel good, sensually, but are destroying our spirit? If we loved ourselves, wouldn't we take care of our bodies? If we loved ourselves, wouldn't we take control of our own minds, that God-given feature He has equipped us all with? Loving ourselves has everything to do with our speech about ourselves and what we believe to be true. The moment we begin to speak life, we will experience a major shift in our overall well-being. Everything about us will begin to grow and expand; whether health, finances,

relationships, or work. Once we begin to speak positivity, notice how everything around us changes. Our circumstances may be the same, but we will see life differently. We will experience more peace, more abundance, and more happiness. We all have greatness inside, begin to live by that.

**Chapter Questions**

What have you been saying about yourself all your life?

Has it been reinforcing or sabotaging your greatness?

When you speak, do you listen carefully to yourself?

Do you pay attention to your words daily?

**Action**

Take inventory of your own heart, by listening to the people you are around, the conversations you engage, the movies you watch, the books you read, and even the music you listen to. Every time you routinely engage in this, you will begin to realize who you are. With everything taken into careful consideration, the total of these thoughts is what comes out of your mouth.

CHAPTER

# 7

# Law of Love

*"And thou shalt love the Lord thy God with all thy heart, and with all thy soul, and with all thy mind, and with all thy strength: this is the first commandment. And the second is like, namely this, thou shalt love thy neighbor as thyself. There is none other commandment greater than these."*
*Mark 12: 30-31.*

The Bible says God is love. We are charged to love one another as ourselves, yet some of us find it hard to love ourselves because of the abuse we have endured throughout life. Everyone experiences troubles, but there is a deeper

meaning to love than we may know. To understand what it means to love, we must first understand the four types of love, from the Greek language, there is Agapē, Phileō, Storgē and Eros.

The highest and most noble form of love is Agapē. Agapē is the type of love that God extends to His children and the world, as stated in John 3: 16, "For God so loved the world that He gave His only begotten Son that whosoever believed in Him should not perish but have everlasting life." Agapē is the type of love that keeps on giving, even when one does not feel worthy or responsive, better known as unconditional love. It stems from being itself and is not based upon any outside circumstances.

Now, we move on to Phileō. Phileō is the type of love that is felt out of companionship. This type of love is normally felt in a friendship or liking of a person's qualities, character, or attributes. It is the type of love that loves to give and receive, and acknowledges appreciation, friendliness, and kindheartedness. Phileō is involved in romantic relationships, as we have heard the phrase, between lovers, "You are my best friend!"

Next is Storgē. Storgē is the type of love that carries a natural affection, or the idea that because of who that

person or thing is. It's a deep feeling that resides inside of us, extending to something or someone close to our hearts. It is the type of love that loving parents extend to their children. We also display this type of love to our pets.

Lastly, there is Eros. Eros is erotic love. It is a passionate love between persons that should be expressed within the confines of marriage. Oftentimes we abuse this type of love because it is a self-satisfying love. It's the type of love that makes someone say, "I love you because you make me smile." It is the type of love that gives to receive. One of the biggest differences between Eros and Phileō, is Phileō is about "us" and Eros is more about "I" or "me." Eros is a conditional type love, based on an attraction to another person.

All the types of love are very important for us to understand as the English language only has one word to describe love and that is the word love itself. We tend to abuse the word because we sometimes overuse it to describe many different expressions.

God commanded us to love one another with the type of love that transcends all conditionings, circumstances, and is very open and honest. Here in the United States, there is a steep decline of compassion for

strangers in any conflict that does not directly affect us. We oftentimes can see this as we drive pass the homeless, ignoring charity, or just flat out refusing to offer help to anyone, regardless the situation. With God's love, we tend to give and show love and compassion unconsciously. I encourage us all to obey God's law of love. It is truly a blessing to be able to give rather than need to receive.

## Chapter Questions

How has God shown His love in your life?

Have you extended love to a stranger recently?

Have you turned yourself away from someone in need?

Is there someone in your immediate family that needs love right now?

How are you displaying God's love in your life?

## Action

Extend love to a stranger, whether a hug or a compliment. If you see someone having a hard time or a bad day, offer words of encouragement. Sometimes we all need to know that someone cares and loves us.

- 42 - | P a g e

CHAPTER

# 8

# Law of Money

*"For where your treasure is, there will your heart be also."*
*Matthew 6:21/Luke 12:34*

Your heart represents your core values, your belief system, and your feelings. The treasure represents your dreams, ambitions, and aspirations, tangible or intangible. Let not your treasure be on things of this world, lest your heart be of this world. In other words, be careful not to go through life seeking things to acquire to affirm yourself. Let not worldly possessions be your focus and drive, but

rather seek the inner truths about yourself and your purpose for being here.

Our beliefs about money can either attract or repel it. Most of us have grew up with limiting beliefs about money, and we've been brainwashed to believe having a lot of money means you're greedy, as well as you possess an evil heart. Quick side note; have you ever heard limiting phrases like *rich people are pigs, happiness is more important than money, or my favorite, "You got McDonald's money?"* If you have heard this or been taught it, you may have limiting beliefs about money. Believe it or not, those beliefs are still working in many of our lives today. To prove this, look at your bank accounts and how you handle investments. Are you good with money and always have it or do you seem to always lose it? Poor-minded believers often quote verses from the Bible without the right context such as Matthew 19:24 and 1 Timothy 6:10 to justify their way of thinking. There's an old song I remember hearing that says, "Silver and gold, I rather have Jesus, than silver and gold." It is understandable to see their point of not sacrificing their souls for worldly possessions, but rather than search for the truth, it is often said to comfort us in our lack mentality. God intended for us to live a good life, filled without worries, including worries

about money. In fact, God gives us the power to attain wealth (see Deut. 8:18). Another popular but untrue saying is, "money is the root of all evil." Being rich is not evil. It is easier to live life with money than without. The Bible says, "For the love of money is the root of all evil…" Meaning money itself is not evil, it's the intent or motive behind the money that defiles or corrupts the person. I used to hear Mark 8:36 like it was a sin to get rich or have money. It says, *"For what shall it profit a man, if he shall gain the whole world and lose his own soul."* Now these verses are repeated as truth without the knowledge of context. The verses are true, but we misuse them and it hurts us in life. I have seen people literally beg God in prayer for bills to be paid or money they needed, but their internal beliefs contradict their sayings. As if God works on emotion and not law. If God worked on emotion, we can appeal to His emotions and get whatever we want, when we want it. We see this with children and some parents. If God gave us everything we asked for, out of emotion, it could literally kill us. The million dollars I asked for in 9th grade, would have killed me. Remember God's laws are designed to govern, guide, and protect us.

The people that repeat these sayings are the same type of people that rely on religion to satisfy their belief on

why being poor is noble. There is no nobility in poverty, especially in the Kingdom of God. God is the King and we are His children. Our Father owns everything; it is His good pleasure to give unto us freely. Here is the issue: He will not violate our free will. Which means because of our limiting beliefs about money or material possessions, we don't get what we think God should give to us, because we believe, subconsciously, we don't deserve more than what we already have.

If anyone desires more money, we must first shift our mindset from poverty-conscious to money-conscious. If anyone is having a problem agreeing, let us validate the purpose for money. Money pays for your food, shelter, clothing, medicine, retirement, travel, education and it sends the Gospel world-wide. To neglect money and its purpose will automatically trigger an impoverished mindset. Checking your money habits will reveal if you are money-conscious or poverty-conscious. Are you normally lacking or normally have an abundance? The results will show your beliefs surrounding money.

Earlier in chapter 2, *Law of Faith*, I mentioned Proverbs 23:7 that says, *"For as he thinketh in his heart, so is he."* This can be applied to money, how we use money, how we

think with money, and what we think about money. From the Bible, we know to judge a tree by its fruit. Most of us have been raised on a middle or working-class income, and we wonder why we sometimes take the same financial routes as our parents. For example, a dog cannot teach a dog how to be a cat, it is outside of its nature. With this truth, we know a poor-minded individual cannot teach someone how to become wealthy, they can only teach what they know; likewise for working or middle class. A poor or middle-class individual cannot teach someone to have a wealthy mindset, unless they themselves first attain a wealthy mindset.

Starting to become money-conscious is simple, but the transformation can be challenging. I suggest repeating affirmations daily, and as often as possible, that will create a wealthy mindset. You can find wealth affirmations in a simple online search. This is the starting point of transformation and belief.

Money is a tool and tools do no work without someone operating it. A car does not drive itself without a person controlling it. Even today, on the brink of self-driving cars, they are still operated by someone ultimately in control. I heard someone say that money is powerless,

and I believe it. It takes on the power and personality of the holder. If you believe in helping in any form or fashion, your money will reflect that. On the other hand, if you are greedy and selfish, the use and behavior of your money will reflect that. Money does not change you, it only magnifies who you already are. Use money to your discretion. If you like to help by giving, do it. If you like to treat yourself to a nice upscale restaurant, do it. If you want to own a $10 million estate, do it! Whatever you do, do it all for the glory of God!

In the Kingdom of God, money is important. Know and believe money is important and it is your duty to acquire wealth, as it reflects well on the King. We must be honest with ourselves and realize money allows us to enjoy more of life. It is easier to attract people and resources when we have money. It is also easier when we have more than we need. Aside from all financial responsibilities, wouldn't it be nice to travel the world, vacation with family, eat at the top restaurants, sleep in the best hotels, live in our dream homes or even give our kids the best education? Money makes all that possible, but thinking we can't have it or don't deserve it will rob us of a good life. Think about it.

## Chapter Questions

How have you been in control of money lately?

Has the pursuit of money ever caused you to lose sight of your morals?

How has money served you lately?

Have you taken the time to learn how to master money?


## Action

Start to keep track of your money. Where you are spending and how much? Have a spreadsheet to keep up with your finances. You will see that wherever you are giving your money, it directly correlates to what you believe. Whether eating at fast-food restaurants or splurging on expensive items, we spend where our hearts are and what we believe about ourselves.

- 50 - | P a g e

CHAPTER

# 9

# Law of Mentorship

*"He who walks with wise men will be wise, But the companion of fools will suffer harm." Proverbs 13:20*

When I decided to become wealthy, there was a shift I had not noticed. Eventually I found myself around people that were already wealthy and successful in their respective careers. One of my first millionaire coaches was my manager at my first job out of college. One of the lessons he taught me was to "Act as if." It means to go at life as if you have everything you want already, as if your life is already amazing and you have accomplished those

things in which your heart desires. One of the quotes he told me that still plays in my head every night before I close my sleepy eyes, "You must be brainwashed for success." I grew up in an environment where most people have lost hope in themselves and their dreams. They would talk about how God was going to do this and going to do that, but it never seemed to happen for them. I remember one night screaming at God because nothing I was trying worked, according to the way I was taught. On that night, God opened my eyes and I began to see life differently. Here I was wanting to be successful and have a life worth living, yet my mental conditioning was set up for financial failure and impoverished thinking. I would often hear friends say, "Everybody ain't able," which really ticked me off since I knew if I could do it, they could as well. At that time, we did not understand the way we were taught affected our lives on a far deeper level than we could imagine. Anything learned can be unlearned, if given the proper time and effort. I decided to spend more time with people far more successful than I was and mimic their behavior, learning how they approached work, and how they viewed life and family. This gave me a new insight on how to approach issues and ultimately brought me more success.

The Bible teaches in Proverbs 2:7, "Iron sharpens iron, so one man sharpens another." To speed up the process and catapult you to success, dumb down your thinking and literally follow successful people. Find out their drives, how they think, how they speak, and how they live. Mentoring has been one of the easiest and quickest ways to success. Your mentors will give you their wisdom based upon their life experiences. You will get a head start, but not a shortcut. Be very careful not to skip through adversity and avoid problems as they are building blocks of character. Shortcuts encourage unjust behavior and actions to obtain your success. Ask yourself, "Do I want success for a moment, or a lifetime? If you chose the latter, I congratulate you in pursuing your dreams and goals and employing a "whatever it takes mentality." Often, mentors will say or do just what you need to be done or said in your life as they want you to succeed. I have not met a mentor that did not want their students to be more successful than they are. They love to succeed and want others to succeed as well. Mentors experience great joy when a student takes their advice, magnifies, and use it to become successful. Mentors often know how to deal with situations you may be facing because they have been there and will share their steps for climbing out of the struggle.

Finding a mentor is easier than you may think. Oftentimes we want God to move faster and give us everything we want when we want it. God has already set our course in motion, all we must do is keep moving, actively seeking your purpose. In my personal experience, once I decided I needed a mentor and began to actively seek them out, that person will literally show up. Have you ever been in a situation where whatever you needed did not come until the exact moment you needed it? That's the way with life, everything you need will come according to its time. Those dreams harboring in your mind will come when they come. Don't rush, just continue to pursue.

Mentors often have more information than a pupil can digest in a year's time. It is very necessary to have a mentor, someone you want to emulate and eventually become at some point in your life. Mentors are forever, you should never stop learning and you should always seek knowledge to become better. Live life with a passion to learn and to grow. Live to become fulfilled as that will be the driving factor for all your actions. Live life to love!

## Chapter Questions

Have you considered a mentor?

What type of mentor would you like?

What type of student would you be?

Are you ready to be pushed to your greatest potential?

How are you looking to advance your life?

## Action

Mentors are not all flesh and blood. Most of my mentors are words written in a book. Begin now to read and find material related to where you want to be spiritually, mentally, financially, and physically. Once you begin this, your mind will shift and soon you will meet people that can be a mentor to you.

- 56 - | Page

CHAPTER

# 10

# Law of Giving

*"But this I say, He which sows sparingly shall reap also sparingly; and he which sows bountifully shall reap also bountifully."*

*2 Corinthians 9:6*

The Spirit of Giving is a beautiful experience. It is open and free and fears no lack. I heard once before, if you are constantly in a mood to give, it means that God is closest to you.

Giving is a law and a commandment from God. God's key to an abundant life is through giving. Giving is

one of the most powerful acts one can commit. The Law of Giving can be referred to as the Law of Sowing and Reaping. The Bible tells us the more we give, the more we can receive. Whenever we give, out of the goodness of our own heart, we are giving to ourselves. We are all interconnected in life. Recall a time when you gave to a stranger, whether money, food, or advice. Ask yourself, how did it make you feel? If you felt good about it, it is because your giving was genuine. Some people will only give to be seen by men. The Bible talks about this when Jesus spoke to his disciples about fasting and praying to not do things so they can be seen of men, but unto the Father. Be careful not to give to be recognized or acknowledged. Our giving should be of a pure heart. The moment we begin to give to be seen and no one is there to see, our giving stops. Giving should be an internal influence, not an external one.

Giving allow us to become more of who we already are. The person who gives more, will receive more than they need and will be able to continually give. Recall the natural laws of physics, where it states, "For every action, there is an equal and opposite reaction." It correlates with, "If you sow abundantly, you will reap abundantly, and if you sow sparingly, you will also reap sparingly." The more

you put into life, the more you contribute, the more you give, then the more you receive, in any area. Giving more of yourself freely expresses more of whom you already are. It is fulfilling and gratifying to experience life on a level of freedom. This is the definition of true success. Being fully who you are and knowing what you are here to accomplish. Everything else will fall into place at the right moment.

The Bible tells us in Luke 6:38, *"Give, and it shall be given unto you; good measure, pressed down, and shaken together, and running over shall men give into your bosom. For with the same measure that ye mete withal it shall be measured to you again."* God's love is directly related to giving. We know that with giving, we could end world hunger and poverty in a single night. Giving often leaves us feeling a sense of gratefulness, being able to give. At its core, giving is truly giving unto one's self. We are also familiar with Karma, or what goes around comes around, or what goes up, must come down. Well, when we give, we are sending out good energy that will be returned to us at a greater measure. We may give money and in return, receive more money or something money cannot buy like peace, love, and true happiness. Most people do not give because they feel they do not have enough. They operate from a scarcity mindset and not abundance, total

opposite of the Kingdom of God. Once you recognize there is no shortage in the Kingdom of God, you will be able to give freely. You want to let the Spirit of Giving flow through you and around you because you will get more of what you give. Do not subject giving to material wealth or possessions only, but giving more of yourself in your work, your relationships, and everything you are involved in. Even when you feel you have nothing to give, give all you have!

For God so loved the world that He *gave* His only begotten son that whosoever believeth in him should not perish but have everlasting life (John 3:16). Know that God *gives* when He needs work done. Know He will provide a way, always.

Above all, give yourself to your dream and purpose in life. We will never accomplish our goals and dreams if we never fully commit to giving it all we have. There is an old saying that goes, "Give it all you've got." Never give up, leave it all on the table, and hold no regrets. This has to be one of the most important ideas to hold to. Literally throw all of yourself into your work. Notice how each wealthy individual got their wealth by doing one thing first. They dedicated their entire beings into becoming the person

of their dreams. Take for example Muhammad Ali, giving his entire life to boxing. It is what he lived for, breathed, and eventually died with. Look among any great contributors of life, they fully gave themselves to their work. We must do the same. Do not be afraid of doing one task for 30 years, just be sure not to be in the same spot-for 30 years. Always be in constant growth and manifestation. When I began to think about what I wanted to do in life, I thought about the people I grew up around and how they were working for the same company for 20, 30, or 40 years and had no ownership. This deterred me from wanting to give myself to one idea or calling in life. I began to research more on ownership and creating my own brand and realized, I can work in a single field, which is my dream, and build it from the ground up. Eventually once you are successful in an area of life, you will become influential in other areas of life as well. It is better to be able to give, than need to receive!

## Chapter Questions

Have you decided to give your all to your dream?

What has stopped you from fully giving to your dream?

How has giving affected your life?

What can you learn from giving?

Who benefits most from giving?

How has God showed His promises through giving?

## Action

Giving is spiritual, it flows to and through us. Begin now to start giving, if you are not already. Giving is not limited to money, but in all areas of life you can give. Give a compliment, give some time, give food, and give more of yourself to your dreams. No matter the amount, just begin to give.

CHAPTER

# 11

# Law of Expectation

*"Jesus said unto him, if thou canst believe, all things are possible to him that believeth."*
*Mark 9:23*

Expectation can be defined as acting in a manner as if something has already happened. When new couples are expecting a baby, they buy a crib, pampers, formula, toys, and other necessities in preparation to accommodate their new arrival. If we are expecting to get a new car, we look at insurance rates, go on test drives, and clean out the garage to make room for the new addition. If you are expecting a huge financial blessing, wouldn't you have a plan on what

to do with the money or how to manage it? Expectation is easily viewed when it is Black Friday and businesses order more products for consumers to meet "expected" demand. I recall walking in Best Buy in Thousand Oaks, California, just two days before Black Friday, and the entire store was fitted with more TVs, Apple products, cameras, just about any electronic one could think of, encompassing the entire store. It was a maze where normally there was open space. I thought to myself, here is the Law of Expectation working before my eyes. Best Buy expected hundreds, if not thousands, of shoppers to pour into their store and buy more than they would on a normal business day. We must also be in expectation with every aspect of our lives, whether business, personal, or financially. Without expectation, there is no manifestation.

Naturally, humans are more developed in expecting the worse than the best. The old saying, "Prepare for the worst, and expect the best," mostly is not true, in the fashion we use it. We focus so much on the negative outcome we never expect the best to happen for us. We must find ourselves in a state of constant expectation of greatness, and set ourselves up for it. It is easy for us to expect negativity daily because we are fed negativity at every turn in life. Our news, social media, speaking habits,

and even our very thoughts about life and ourselves are innately negative. It is easier for a human to believe negatively than positively.

We can measure expectation by what we are doing. When we say, "I want to achieve this, or I want a car like that, or I want to have this type of lifestyle," based upon our actions, we can achieve that goal. "Wants" show up in conversation, expectation arrives in behavior. We will know what to expect based upon our behavior and actions. Which, reflecting, is why the Bible says judge a tree by its fruit. We normally get caught up in proclamations and sayings, but never actually put the work in. God looks at our hearts. We do much speaking with our mouths but lack the expectation and action to receive it. Once again, where there is no expectation, there is no manifestation.

The Bible states, *"For we walk by faith and not by sight." 2 Corinthians 5:7.* When we are in expectation, our vision becomes greater than our obstacles. Naturally, life may not be yielding favorable results presently, but spiritually, we have faith that the problem is solved or the issue has been worked out.

We receive what we expect, internally. If we develop negativity, we will speak, expect, and receive

negativity. Also, the antithesis is true. Once positivity is developed, we will speak and think positively and receive positive results. Earl Nightingale said famously, "Our lives move in the direction of our currently dominant thoughts." Dominate your life by controlling your thoughts and expect the best whether spiritually, emotionally, mentally, physically, and financially.

## Chapter Questions

What are you expecting to happen in your life?

What have you been neglecting to expect and not yet received?

Are you willing to endure disappointment and setbacks while you are expecting your dream to manifest?

Are you capable of recognizing your short-comings with expectation?

Do your values reflect your expectations in life?

## Action

Live life expecting good things to happen to you. At every turn, expect your affairs to succeed, expect people to give unto you, expect life to yield to your ambitions. Expect greatness, work for greatness, and achieve greatness.

- 68 - | P a g e

CHAPTER

# 12

# Law of Management

*"He that is faithful in that which is least is faithful also in much." Luke 16: 10*

If you ever found yourself thinking about what you do not have or why you do not have what you want, take a deep look at your management skills, otherwise known as stewardship. Every person has exactly what they can handle at this very moment. God loves us so much He will keep us at the level we can handle rather than give us what we think we want; it is detrimental to our well-being. Gaining more riches in your lifetime heavily depends upon

handling your current affairs. Almost everyone wants more money, love, freedom, and peace, but fail to realize we are the only ones holding ourselves back.

When there is a desire to advance in life, God always checks the management ability. Many people would pray for a million dollars but cannot handle managing a thousand. We must understand that part of our free will is the ability to choose how we allocate resources. God gives us the ability to think and act for ourselves. We should use our abilities to advance ourselves and our communities. Quickly, think about the type of person you are with money. Are you a saver or spender? Some people never consciously manage their resources. We impulse buy, go out every chance we get, or sometimes literally try to not spend money, but the opportunities to spend are always there. I was only broke because I would spend every single dime I had. If my bank account had $3.42 in it, I would get three dollar-menu items and with the taxes, my account would hit zero. I lived my life this way since I first started dealing with money, often being at zero or carrying a negative balance. Twice my bank account was closed because I carried a negative balance for more than 40 days. I despised my monetary ways and hated checking my account balance, because it would always be very low. I

would wonder why I could never keep money and literally hide money from myself, until I found it. Then, I would spend it. I blamed it on every excuse I could find. It was never my fault. What I found was that I did not know about my role in managing my own resources. We must understand, once we take control of our own lives and own our money habits and make an effort to consciously improve them, then our money will reflect a positive change.

The Law of Management also pertains to how we treat others' resources, and behave on our jobs. Recall the parable in Matthew 25:14-30, where the master leaves his servants each with a measure of talents. He gives one five, another two, and the last, he gives one. The first two traded and doubled what they were given and the last buried his talent and upon the master's return gave it back to him. The master called him a wicked and lazy servant and had him tossed out of his presence. Notice how the two servants that doubled what they were given was given more and the lazy servant lost what he was given. The same with resources we are given and are expected to increase, including our gifts we received before birth.

We must realize we are being watched and measured, daily. God sees everything we do, in every aspect of life. He keeps notice of how we perform and our ability. We receive according to our ability to manage. No one should ever be jealous of someone else because of what they have; each of us can increase what we already have. When we find ourselves looking to what we lack, we can change it by being more effective in managing what we already have and then we shall increase.

God also takes notice of how we treat another person's property. The Bible says, "If you cannot be trusted with another man's, who will give you your own?" If you have a job, be very careful not to break the law of management. This means, showing up to work late, stealing time to get paid more, taking things from the job, misusing company resources. We can get caught in "the company won't miss this," and take what does not belong to us. God watches it all and depending on how you manage others, will determine if you'll get your own.

Most people do not realize whatever we put into our work, is what we get out of it. There are some who refuse to go the extra-mile on a job. They say things like, "I don't get paid enough for this." That type of thinking will keep us

in an unwanted state of being. There is an old saying, "Do more than what you are paid to do, and soon you will be paid more than what you do." Going the extra-mile on a job will produce the habit that will carry us for the rest of our lives. Imagine going the extra-mile on your own business. How much more would you be able to accomplish doing what you love if you build the habit now? Not going the extra-mile simply keeps us in a place we do not want to be. This leads to frustration and eventually leaving the job, but failing to recognize the change must be within ourselves.

We all want more out of life. Management is crucial to our futures. We should always keep in mind we are being measured for greatness at every point. Begin now to actively manage your resources and the resources you have been trusted with. Then one day, you shall have our own, and others will manage for you.

## Chapter Questions

Have you been negating your own advancement?

How can you become a more effective money manager?

Can anyone trust you with their property?

Do you trust yourself with your current wealth?

## Action

Use what you have in your possession to increase your abilities. Money is an easy start. Build a money plan. There are a few to follow. Two I'll mention is the JARS System and the 70-10-10-10 System I heard about from Jim Rohn. Personally, I use a mixture of both and they can be found online. I urge you to research them.

# Conclusion

All divine laws coincide with each other. They are symbiotic. The Bible says all things work together for the good of those that love him and are called according to His purpose (Romans 8:28). God had specific instructions on why laws should be followed. The Bible states in Joshua 1:8, "This book of the law shall not depart out of thy mouth; but thou shalt meditate therein day and night, that thou mayest observe to do according to all that is written therein: for then thou shalt make thy way prosperous, and then thou shalt have good success." This law is still

relevant today when we focus on the laws and how they operate. It says *you* shall make *your* way prosperous. God gives us the ability to control our lives and the directions we want to go. The laws are set up to guide us to making our lives free and beautiful, to create happiness.

Deuteronomy 8:18 states, *"It is the Lord that gives the power to get wealth."* God is all about success, in every form. If it were not so, birds wouldn't fly on their own, fish couldn't swim, and seeds would not yield trees. We are literally built to succeed; it is already in us. Think about all the accomplishments and advances we have achieved, the greatness we have seen from now back to the beginning of time. The earth is the Lord's and the fullness thereof. Anything that has anything to do with God, following His laws, will be successful. We could all agree that the world is very rich, regardless of who owns what. There are riches that have not been yet discovered, untold riches. As this earth remains, and God is God, this planet, the laws, and everything here shall be in abundance and remain.

God's laws are designed to help everyone achieve success in every area of life. Success in their health, finances, professional relationships, careers, and the list goes on. It is up to us to identify what success looks like for us and let the laws of God work in our favor. Think about

- 76 - | P a g e

the qualities of Heaven and ask yourself, is there any famine, lack, or scarcity? The obvious answer is no, there is not any, but here on earth, we fall victim to worry and fear and forget what God says. God's laws produce joy, peace, happiness, love, and forgiveness. Galatians 5: 22-23 says, *"But the fruit of the Spirit is love, joy, peace, longsuffering, gentleness, goodness, faith, meekness, and temperance."* We pray, "…thy will be done on earth, as it is in Heaven." We have the ability and resources to make our lives Heaven on Earth. To experience life more abundantly, and to capture to full essence of what it means to be alive    living a fulfilled life.

Lastly, recall in 3 John 1: 2, "Beloved, I wish above all things that thou may prosper and be in health, even as thy soul prospers." Be prosperous, and enjoy life. Understand that we are literally built to win!

- 78 - | Page

# About the Author

A graduate of Xavier University of Louisiana, Kevin Wayne Joseph aims to target anyone that is struggling with figuring out *why*? As his first body of work, he hopes this book will open eyes, transform lives, and unlock dreams that are lying dormant. Kevin has a passion for motivation and often looks for opportunities to share his gift, motivate others, and give hope to anyone feeling down. He has helped start Agrowtopia, an urban farm on Xavier's campus, that provides fresh, affordable produce to the local communities to combat food deserts. Kevin wants to inspire others to achieve their dreams.

- 80 - | P a g e

Made in the USA
Columbia, SC
29 July 2017

Made in the USA
Middletown, DE
18 June 2021

Book One: Purpose

## Resource page

**Website**

https://www.rainn.org/

RAINN is the nation's largest anti-sexual violence organization.

**Books**

Victims No Longer; *Mike Lew*

Black Pain. It Just Looks Like We're Not Hurting; *Terri M Williams*

Book One: Purpose